Challenges
in
Later Life

MARY THREADGOLD RSC

First published in 2017 by Messenger Publications

ISBN 978 1 910248 68 3

Designed by Messenger Publications Design Department
Typeset in Times New Roman and Minion Pro
Printed by Nicholson & Bass Ltd.

Messenger Publications,
37 Lower Leeson Street, Dublin D02 W938
www.messenger.ie

CONTENTS

As a child, the love of my life was my grandfather. From infancy, along with my father and brother, I had lived with extended family which included grandparents, uncles and an aunt. My mother had died shortly after I was born. Granda and I were besotted with one another; this was my first experience of unconditional love, which has stood me in good stead spiritually. I could do nothing wrong, and he was faultless in my eyes. This was a good model for, and introduction to, our Heavenly Father and the concept of divine compassion.

Granda was left an orphan in 1870. His parents died in an epidemic – either flu or cholera. They were buried in 'the cabbage plot' which was an emergency graveyard with no headstones. We never found their burial spot. He was fostered to distant relatives and grew up in Glenasmole, Dublin where the seeds of the faith must have been sown.

The Granda that I knew in the 1940s and 1950s was a man of deep faith. He used a prayer book to pray early each morning. He sauntered down every day to the parish church in Dalkey for 10 a.m. Mass, arriving in time to make the Stations of the Cross before Mass commenced. In the evening time, when the Angelus was rung by the parish church, he would find my brother and I wherever we were playing and call us to come with him to the bedroom where there was a picture of the Sacred Heart. There we would say the Angelus with him. After tea, we all kneeled and he led us in the rosary. He was a regular attender at sodality meetings. He didn't smoke and he rarely drank anything stronger than cider (which was his Christmas Day treat).

He never preached religion and he never read spiritual books, except perhaps an odd CTS booklet or missionary magazine, but he was a man of God. Granda was the embodiment of the faith. It may be comforting for grandparents to realise that the loving example they give to their grandchildren does rub off and, although the seeds of faith may not blossom immediately, indeed they may take a long time to bear fruit, our hope is that in due course they will.

In reflecting upon what I would include in this booklet, I decided to cast the net wide and look at the many challenges that impact upon the lives of older people today. Whether those have to do with physical difficulties or the social, intellectual, emotional or spiritual complexities that effect our lives in the twenty-first century.

Who is the intended audience of this booklet? It is for those of us who grew up in the 1940s or earlier. I believe that we have a lot of valuable information to share which can help others deal with issues that occur on several levels as we age. Our life experiences demonstrate both our resilience and our limitations in coping with all that life presents to us. This booklet is also for those who care for, or care about, older people in wider society. This includes relatives, friends and carers. It is hoped that in reading this booklet they will gain additional insights into the challenges facing older people today, and how they might approach helping those in their lives facing these challenges.

For older people, nothing is really simple. Those activities which younger generations take for granted, at some point become enormous in the risks they can pose to us. Physical challenges like arthritis, or other causes of reduced mobility, often have an emotional or psychological overlay too (which can accentuate the physical challenges) as we experience the loss of the agility that we once took for granted. Social issues like loneliness are closely related to physical limitations when we are not able to leave the house to meet old friends or mix in social circles like day centres or active retirement groups. Further to this, for many of us, spiritual and emotional issues often overlap to create multiple levels of risk to our well-being.

Before moving on I would like you, the reader, to think about the issues that bother you. Then you can see how these can be helped by the suggestions contained herein.

Physical Challenges

A re you the kind of person who has various health challenges, with added frailty and perhaps some difficulties in accessing or consuming medication as prescribed as a result? Maybe you have mobility problems due to a stroke, or arthritis, or a fall which resulted in a fracture. Falls undermine the confidence of many older people, even without a resultant fracture. You may have friends who have hearing problems, or issues with their hearing aids; others might have sight problems. Then there are the typical gamut of age-related issues like fatigue, obesity and sight problems possibly complicated by a poor sleep pattern. Noise adds to many problems including getting to sleep. For those with hearing difficulties who use hearing aids, background noise can be very disturbing. Inadequate nutrition can follow as a result of a bad habit of eating snacks during the day, instead of more nourishing meals at regular times.

There are myriad physical challenges related to the outside world that we have to navigate. These might include the state of the pavements or the presence of other hazards, such as building works, putting you at risk of falling. Public transport has its problems too, such as having to stand while you wait a long time for a bus or other transportation; stepping up and down as you enter or leave a bus can be difficult, also the jerking of the bus as it starts or stops can knock you off balance.

Reduced availability of ready cash in many banks is causing problems for many older people who also find that they receive limited assistance in public offices or hospitals. Crowds in public places, together with the attendant cacophony of noise, make life unpleasant and, for those living in a care setting, unwanted television or choice of programme can be very trying.

Suggestions that might help

What can you do to reduce the effects of physical difficulties? Taking care of your general health comes high on the list. This includes a balanced diet and adequate nutrition, eating regularly and sensibly. If a meal delivery service is available, make sure to arrange for them to be delivered if you are not able to go shopping or manage the cooking yourself. Learn to handle medication and use the systems that have been developed, such as blister packs, to remind you when to take your tablets. Your local pharmacist will be able to offer you excellent advice on this. Exercise and fresh air are important and worth the effort that you might have to make to leave the comfort of your home.

There are endless physical supports available such as a walking stick, a walking frame, pressure cushions, standing poles and other mobility aids. If your hearing or sight are deteriorating, be sure to avail of whatever devices you need. Public health nurses are a font of knowledge for older people, and are usually more than happy to offer advice on getting the right supports. Short rests can be helpful, or even necessary, to maintain your energy throughout the day as long as they don't interfere with you getting an adequate night's sleep.

Finding ourselves and our physical challenges in the gospels

When Jesus was engaged in his public ministry he often encountered people with physical problems, such as the man with the withered hand. You will find this in *Matthew 12:9-13*, or the man crippled for thirty-eight years, which you can find in *John 5:1-8*. You will find Peter's mother-in-law, when she had a fever, in *Luke 4:38-40*. It is very easy to find gospel references through internet search providers (Google or Bing, for example) if you or your family are internet users. Type in 'scripture incident' and add a few words to describe the incident (e.g. Peter's mother-in-law), and you should get relevant results.

Why not take one of these passages, read it slowly, imagine you are there too and, when it comes to your turn for Jesus to come near and catch your eye, tell him what is the matter with you and how you feel about it. If he doesn't touch you and heal you, talk to him or Our Lady, and ask for healing or patience in illness. Remember that Our Lady went to Jesus and said, 'They have no wine', so perhaps she would do the same for you and say something like, 'He/she has a pain in his/her hip' or, 'He/she can't get a proper night's sleep', thereby invoking Jesus' blessing for you.

You then play your part by living with your condition as it effects you in the present and asking for the grace to be patient while you wait for things to improve. It can be helpful to adopt the attitude of allowing yourself to feel the discomfort of the disability instead of fighting against it. That can lead to greater acceptance which, in turn, can contribute to a reduction or a resolution of your problem. Never forget that physical health and mental health are inextricably linked, and an improvement in one may well lead to an improvement in the other.

✎ SECTION 2 ✎
Social Challenges

Many older people experience loneliness or have relationship issues, either with some family members or other unresolved relationships. There can be separate family issues to do with finance, property or wills and testaments. These all detract from the peace of mind that is so essential to your well-being, especially in later life. Another issue can be due to the fact that one's social circle is shrinking as a result of death or incapacity of friends and acquaintances. Positive relationships with adult children, and grandchildren, are a joy to many older people but that can be tempered somewhat by the number of grandparents who are asked to provide babysitting or childminding services for their families. A little is welcomed, but older people tire easily and sometimes too much is expected of them. One grandmother that I spoke to whilst writing this booklet felt very frustrated by grandchildren who came to visit, but immediately became engrossed in their technical devices.

At another level, older people can frequently feel that they are not being treated with respect. In its worst form this can constitute elder abuse. Often there is nobody to give them time, to listen to them or share memories with them. There can be a lack of humour and laughter in their lives. For some, it causes distress if they are addressed inappropriately, such as someone using their first name when they would prefer a more formal form of address or vice-versa.

It is very important to recognise that, as an older person, they need help. Some are unwilling to accept help either from family or acquaintances despite the fact that it is readily available to them, either informally or through the public health or social welfare systems. This might include refusing to accept meal delivery services or attendance at a day or health centre. They might also refuse the services of home help or other types of domestic care.

Older people can find social attitudes upsetting. Either because they are too liberal (often a feature of the younger age groups) or too traditional and inflexible (often a feature of their own peer group). Others can have rigid expectations in relation to them, for example if they live in a nursing home and they have to be present in the dining room for breakfast when they would love a lie-in in bed.

Suggestions that might help

It is so helpful and invigorating when you find a friendly person to have a conversation with, somebody who has time to listen and is interested in you as a person. Quality interaction, and engagement from all involved, is the key to satisfactory conversation(s). Since loneliness is both a social and emotional issue, we will explore it more extensively in the section on emotional challenges. Having time with grandchildren and other younger people, and sharing your own stories with them, can be a blessed experience.

In some nursing homes reminiscence sessions are held by the activity organiser. These bring back memories at a social level, but the opportunity to share old family photographs and memories with an interested family member or close friend can be even more comforting. Some, though not all, like to take part in the sing-songs and parties available. All the better if these involve younger people, as inter-generational sessions can offer a special dimension and energy to the occasion.

Finally, pets should be considered seriously. They are great companions. Dogs and cats have different qualities to offer a would-be owner. Dogs may be more expensive to maintain whether it is the cost of dog food, vet visits or grooming. They also need regular exercise, sometimes intensive, which can be a problem if the older person has limited mobility, unless alternatives can be found for dog walking. However, they are such loyal and loving companions and have reduced loneliness in many lives. I recently read in a daily paper that older people are happier if they have 'something to do, someone to love and something to look forward to'. Animals, especially dogs, are there to love and be loved, especially for people living on their own.

Cats on the other hand require lower maintenance. There will still be vet bills and cat food bills but they are very self-sufficient creatures, while at the same time offering company and affection to the housebound person. Cats have their own way of taking exercise, so therefore they require less rigorous attention.

Some older people have a liking for birds. They can be attractive both for their colour and their song. Parrots can be amusing if taught particular phrases. A fish tank is also an option, although help may be required in the maintenance of it as it can be an arduous task depending on its size.

Finding ourselves and our social challenges in the gospels

When Our Lady and a group of acquaintances tried to get to see Jesus he seemed to detach himself in a way that may have been hurtful *(Matthew 12:48)*. If family takes no interest in their older relative they might feel as we expected Mary to feel – a bit rejected.

Now it's your turn to take this passage. Read it slowly, see yourself as part of the event, see yourself getting the opportunity to talk to Jesus and tell him all about your family or other relationships. Either express gratitude for their kindness, pray for their special needs or seek the grace to forgive a particular hurt.

Then you play your part by living with the situation as it effects you in the present and either asking for the grace to be patient while you wait for things to improve, or thanking God for the way(s) that you have been helped by others. It can be helpful to adopt the attitude of allowing yourself to feel the discomfort of the family situation or other uncomfortable relationships instead of fighting against them. That can lead to greater acceptance which, in turn, can contribute to the resolution of your problem, if there is a problem.

Intellectual/mental Challenges

If you were asked, 'When was the last time you couldn't remember somebody's name?' or, 'When was the last time you went upstairs to get something and, by the time you reached the top of the stairs, couldn't remember what you were looking for?', what would your answers be? For many older people the answer to these questions would be: 'Very recently'. We tend to call these incidents 'senior moments' and, for most of us, that is exactly what they are. They are part and parcel of the normal ageing process. More serious lapses of memory will be discussed later in the booklet but for now, keep in mind, that memory is one of the functions of the brain we treasure. The ability to recall significant and particularly happy times as we look back on our lives is invaluable, so doing what you can to stimulate your memory is absolutely worth the time and effort it may take to do so.

Another essential function of the brain is attention and concentration. As we get older we find it more difficult to maintain the focus of our attention whether this is to do with reading, watching television or doing puzzles such as crosswords. We tend to do a bit, go away and come back to it.

As older people, we have the ability to learn but there is a lot of learning involved in the case of computers and modern telephones (smartphones). Many of us envy younger people who seem to take to this naturally; many older people stop at the first hurdle and have no ambition to go beyond the basics – 'I can take a call and make a call and that's enough for me'. On the other hand, many older people have close relatives who have gone to live abroad. The opportunity to see them and talk to them (for free) may tempt older people to learn how to use Skype, Google Hangouts or Facetime. Another related issue is managing CD players, TV stations and DVD players. These can pose technical problems, and a certain level of perseverance is required on the part of the older person in order to master them, or to be forthcoming in asking for help.

The modern system of accessing services by phone can make for a frustrating experience. You are told, 'Thank you for holding, your call is important to us'. This can raise the blood pressure when you have heard it for the tenth time in one sitting, and that is after being transferred through a range of options to the operator that you needed to speak to in the first place. (It is worth bearing in mind that this frustration isn't borne by older people alone however!) A way of dealing with this may be to revert to a letter or e-mail to the organisation concerned, this also gives you the benefit of a record for future reference. Completing forms can be the dread of many people's lives. The attention to detail required – for census forms for example, or in applying for a medical card, or other service to which you are entitled – can be a significant challenge to an older person.

As older people, we tend to have more difficulty in problem-solving. Often we don't think as clearly as we once did and, when something doesn't work, for example the vacuum cleaner, it might take longer for us to realise that the contents of the internal bag need to be emptied, despite this being a rather routine affair.

In the case of some older people, mention needs to be made of those living with conditions such as dementia, Parkinson's disease or the communicative and physical aspects of a stroke. This can make life very difficult for the person concerned as well as their carers. Support is essential for these people, and it is available through various support groups such as the Alzheimer Society of Ireland, The Irish Heart Foundation or The Parkinson's Association of Ireland, to name but a few. Language can also be a barrier to progression when older person and carers/personal assistants do not speak the same first language (English, for example).

Suggestions that might help

It is important to maintain a positive attitude in the face of everyday difficulties. This can start with acknowledging the issue(s) and a determination to accept the reality of what you have to deal with. Looking to others, including professionals, for either moral support or counselling should always be considered an option. As we get older we tend to become more tolerant, but this varies with differences in personality. People who are perfectionist or anxious may find it more difficult to make allowances for others, or for the daily challenges that face them.

It can help if we see the need to retain our interests and skills. These can vary from cooking and baking to card playing, to the daily crossword, to knitting and maybe, for some, it would include playing golf (or for others, bingo!). Reminiscence and sharing memories can be helpful, either with a familiar individual or in a group setting such as sessions held in day centres. As part of this, you might compile a life-story journal of your own or build a memory box from old items to be found in the attic or put away in drawers. A memory box can be a great source of conversation. The healing power of reminiscence should not be underestimated, even when the times remembered contain hurt and bitterness. For those whose sight is affected, audiobooks are available from libraries or the internet, just as loop systems are available for those with hearing problems.

Many older people enjoy reading, whether it is fiction, fact or poetry. A book of the poems we learned at school can provide comforting memories. Many older people prefer radio programmes to television, especially documentaries or 'Sunday miscellany' where many individuals share their reflections and memories, often in a humorous way. The importance of establishing and sticking to routines cannot be overestimated. They provide a rhythm and pattern to one's day-to-day living that can relieve anxiety and fill what may be an otherwise long day. Learning to utilise Podcasts or online video players on a laptop or tablet can give more choice alongside the usual radio or TV options.

For the more serious memory or communicative problems referred to, professional help may be needed. The local public health nurse can often be a good informational resource, as they will be familiar with local services. Of course, one's GP is also a key person for finding the best way to address the memory and communicative problems of those needing help.

Finding ourselves and our related intellectual challenges in the gospels

When Zechariah was struck dumb at the time of the announcement of the coming of John the Baptist *(Luke 1:18-22)* he had to be patient and to accept his loss of speech while waiting for his son (John the Baptist) to be born. John was later to fulfil an important role in introducing Jesus at the beginning of his public ministry. We have already met the man whose speech was affected through deafness *(Mark 7:31-37)*. Non-verbal communication (i.e. communicating through body language, facial expression or tone of voice without using words) is evident during the Passion when Jesus turned and looked on Peter *(Luke 22:61)*.

Now imagine yourself in this scene. Wait until Jesus comes to you and catches your eye. Tell him what's bothering you and wait for him to respond. You might not hear the answer immediately; maybe it will come when you are out shopping, or washing the dishes or digging the garden.

Turn to Our Lady. We know of some incidents in the gospels when she had to wait until Jesus knew it was the right time to answer her. One was at the marriage feast of Cana, when Mary just told Jesus, 'they have no wine' and he didn't seem to be listening, but we know that he acted later according to her wishes. Tell Mary what you are waiting for from Jesus.

Then you play your part by living with the situation as it effects you in the present and either asking for the grace to be patient while you wait for things to improve, or thanking God for the way you have been helped by others. It can be helpful to adopt the attitude of allowing yourself to feel the discomfort of your poor memory, or your boredom, instead of fighting against it. That can lead to greater acceptance which, in turn, can contribute to a resolution of your problem if there is a problem.

Emotional Challenges

For older people, there are many issues that can make them feel fearful and insecure such as personal security, financial stress and fear of loss, either of their own independence, or that of a loved one. As physical abilities and mental agility are reduced, many older people feel less confident in dealing with challenges that arise in ordinary daily life.

Everyday choices (i.e. personal autonomy) are reduced for many, especially if they are in a nursing home or care environment. This can detract from a person's self-esteem and result in feelings of dejection or, in some cases, frustration or anger as they have to endure unwanted television programmes, or very high volume so as to accommodate others with hearing impairment. Often people experience a lack of consideration, either from their own family members or from carers who do not know them well. At the same time, it is important to admit that our expectations of others may be too high and it is good to be aware of mood problems that are present, like irritability or feelings of dejection.

While reminiscing has many positive effects, and sharing memories can be a positive experience which encourages positive change, it may also trigger feelings of sadness. Allowing ourselves to feel sad is not necessarily a bad thing and often there are tears that *need* to be shed. However, if these feelings persist, further action may need to be taken.

One may need to acknowledge, however begrudgingly, the level of one's sadness and seek appropriate help from friends or professionals. If it is relatively mild, it may be best to meet up with a trusted friend to share how you feel, knowing that you will be listened to respectfully and helpfully. If it is more serious, you may need the professional help of a counsellor (or similar therapist) who may even need to refer you for further medical advice depending their assessment of your mental state.

The same scale applies to other suppressed feelings such as anger, anxiety or resentment and the need to have an understanding and supportive listener at those times. If you feel in relative control of these feelings, then a sympathetic ear from a friend may be all you need, but if these feelings are escalating to an extent that you feel unable to function as a result of them, please feel encouraged to seek a professional's opinion.

Lack of privacy can cause distress. This can be particularly thorny when it comes to sensitive issues such as personal care or financial matters. In some cases, family members may not be able to provide the requisite support, perhaps because of living at a distance, or due to poor interpersonal relationships, or due to a conflict of interest. Making your distress known to the person in charge can demand trust on your part but should be explored as an option.

Some physical conditions interfere with the ability to express needs, wishes or preferences. Speech can be affected by hearing loss, stroke or other serious medical conditions. The mental result of these phsyical ailments is frustration on the part of the older person as well as the listener. The services of a speech and language therapist may be needed and can be accessed through the public health service, such as your GP, or privately.

Mental health issues must be mentioned here. If depression or mood problems, due to an inability to communicate, become a cause of concern, professional help should be sought.

In the early stages of dementia there can be evidence of paranoia when the older person is suspicious that others, including family members, are stealing from them. Finally, there may be occasions when the older person feels bullied. This can happen, even involving family members. It is sometimes serious and at the level of elder abuse.

Accepting weakness and immobility

Physical conditions, including immobility or generalised weakness, need to be seen as part of your life but it is *not* the condition that defines you. You may be familiar with the Serenity Prayer, where one prays to know the difference between the things that can be changed and those conditions that have to be accepted. Very often it takes a medical expert to decide what can be treated and where to get treatment. Following up on expert advice isn't always straightforward due to cost, waiting lists or transport difficulties. Having a support network of family or friends can mean a lot at a time like this.

Having done all that is humanly possible to resolve the problem you may still have to accept what you are left with. Developing a positive attitude and making the best of the situation will reduce your level of discomfort.

Constructing routines that help you through the day will occupy you productively. These routines could include prayer times (Angelus, rosary, CDs such as Ciúnas; or religious TV such as EWTN, where Mass is available daily). Some local churches may broadcast Masses on the parish website. Some parishes have Simon of Cyrene groups who visit housebound people to give them spiritual support. Your routines could also include light chores and telephone calls to friends or to the Senior Help Line, run by the Third Age Foundation, if appropriate.

Above and beyond the challenges already mentioned, loneliness could be considered the most serious issue for many older people. There is a difference between *being alone* and *feeling lonely*. The former is about circumstances, either physical or social; the latter is about how you feel emotionally or psychologically. When you are lonely you feel sad, lack energy and vitality, and carry a certain weariness of spirit, often accompanied by daytime fatigue.

Sometimes people compensate with excessive alcohol consumption, prescription drugs, watching TV excessively, especially soap operas, or by staying in bed. Loneliness can be a side effect of the barriers erected over the years to protect ourselves from the world, or the world from us, due to a lack of trust.

Loneliness has many roots, and absence of companionship can occur through loss, lack of access (e.g. reduced mobility), a shortage of money or being a carer (especially to an older spouse or relative). This can result in a poor social life. It can happen when moving to a new area, especially if that means returning to one's country of origin at the time of retirement. Or perhaps, in some cases, friends and siblings are dying, acquaintances are moving; family is migrating, or moving far away. The attendant problems associated with loneliness are heightened further if there is a hearing or sight problem in the mix, as is often the case.

Events that trigger loneliness include Christmas, anniversaries and birthdays but also songs and music. Another trigger would be coming across the belongings of somebody who is no longer nearby, or who has passed away.

Suggestions that might help

Many of us are not good at discussing our feelings, especially when feeling vulnerable, but it is important for peace of mind to be able to identify and acknowledge what we feel, and then try to express and share this with others. This is where close friends or trusted family members have an important role to play in our lives. This is particularly important where there is a lack of forgiveness and sometimes the forgiveness needs to be for ourselves. Most people become more tolerant as they advance in age. Reviewing one's own tolerance level is a worthwhile exercise, as well as being willing to try to put oneself in the shoes of the person who is bothering you and considering their perspective.

Some people are blessed with a very positive outlook. But if the opposite is true, negativity can cause a lot of other emotional problems that result in degraded peace of mind. We all need things to look forward to, or that we get excited about. If the older person is promised a visit or regular contact, they will likely be looking forward to this immensely. Make sure to keep all such promises so that the older person is not let down and negativity reinforced. Focussing on gratitude is something that pays off where positivity is concerned.

A number of steps can be taken to ward off feelings of loneliness. Having a few close friends is a good start, but in some cases people need to make new friends by participating in local activities like active age groups or day centres. One lady I spoke to was reluctant to attend a day centre and, on the first day, she neither spoke nor ate. By the time I met her some time afterwards she was a happy participant in all that was going on. Building routines into your day can also help so that you live in the present, instead of being sad over losses or your reduced circle of friends. It can also help for you to be mindful of the fact that you may be fighting the feelings of loneliness. By allowing yourself to feel the discomfort that it causes you, acquaint yourself with it and the feeling will lose some of the power it may have wielded over you.

Finally we need to check on our ability to let go. Often we don't realise the extent to which we hold on to things – we hold on to attitudes, feelings, resentments, prejudices, ways of doing things and often, unless we are challenged, we remain unaware that this is so. Even when we are aware, we have to ask ourselves, do we want to let go? Unless we gain more insight into ourselves, become more mindful and instil in ourselves a belief that we need to change for the better, we will not change. If we want to grow emotionally and spiritually we need to accept the fact that nobody owes us anything and we must challenge ourselves not to blame anybody for our feelings. These are difficult principles to live by, but they result in untold blessings, especially the blessing of inner freedom and peace.

Finding ourselves and our related emotional challenges in the gospels

An example of loss in the gospels can be seen in the grief of the widow who lived in Naim and whose only son died *(Luke 7:11-17)*. This is the kind of death that affects many older people who grieve the loss of a loved one. On another occasion, Lazarus died *(John 11:1-44)* and his two sisters, Martha and Mary, were inconsolable until Jesus intervened. Another incident that also began with a death, but which changed to a celebration, was when Mary Magdalen met Jesus in the Garden after his death *(John 20:11-18)*.

Imagine yourself in one of these scenes. Feel the grief at losing one who was dearly loved by you. In the first case, stand beside the widow and experience her grief followed by her joy when her son was restored to her. Think of losses that you have come to terms with and maybe when you have come to the stage where you are thankful for the gift of that person in life. As the crowds disperse you find yourself alone with Jesus – tell him about your heartbreaks. Listen to what he has to say to you and, if he does not give you a measure of consolation immediately, wait until you realise that you have a new insight of your own, and a measure of consolation in relation to what you might have lost.

Turn to Our Lady. She experienced great loss when Jesus died. Talk to her about what she felt then, and tell her how you too have felt. Rejoice with her at the Resurrection and ask her to help you to be hopeful for the present and the future.

Then you play your part by living with the situation as it effects you in the present, and either asking for the grace to be patient while you wait for things to change, or thanking God for the way you have been helped by others. It can be helpful to adopt the attitude of allowing yourself to feel the discomfort of your disappointments or loneliness instead of fighting against these. Acceptance can lead to greater relaxation which, in turn, can contribute to the resolution of your problem, if there is a problem.

⌒ SECTION 5 ⌒
Spiritual Challenges

Spirituality has the potential to help people find meaning in the lives they have lived. In the right environment, which needs to be quiet and uninterrupted, they can be given the opportunity to reflect and make sense of their life experiences. A technique called Spiritual Reminiscence has a contribution to make here (see appendices).

For many people, spirituality is centred on religion, religious observance, religious symbols, practice and prayers. For such people, their relationship with God is a primary concern. For some people who prefer not to have a church affiliation, they see spirituality principally as a relationship with self, others and nature including *the universe*. Older people who are religious can include this set of relationships dealing with self, others and nature, to add to their primary relationship with God. There are also those who relate to a *higher being* as is the case with Alcoholics Anonymous. A well-known figure like Einstein would say that 'kindness, beauty and truth' are the ideals that lit his way and time after time given him new courage to face life cheerfully. These ideals are very close to the Christian ethos.

In either case, harmony in the home and loving relationships go a long way to creating a lived-in spiritual environment. Having time to listen to each other respectfully, showing kindness and consideration, making allowances and being tolerant create conditions where spirituality is alive and can thrive. Added to this, a regard for the natural environment can be brought into day-to-day life with flowers, green spaces, gardening activities and generally uplifting environments. These too are aspects of spirituality.

For the purpose this booklet we will look at particular challenges that concern the older person for whom religion is important. Due to physical or cognitive limitations many people miss the opportunity to attend religious services regularly. In some cases this is because they are not available in their area or within reasonable reach – religious support can be missing. Whereas the older person might have played an active part in parish life in the past, they may now be housebound or in a care/assisted-living situation, which makes it difficult to continue this. In the past they might have enjoyed going on pilgrimages, now that is no longer possible. Some of the symbols of religion may be available to them – they may have holy water and rosary beads, but miss out on statues, holy pictures, prayer books and religious magazines. They are very dependent on the kindness of like-minded people when it comes to having their spiritual and religious needs met.

Keeping an open mind can be helpful, and not allowing opinions and valued attitudes to become frozen and static. Some people can become influenced too easily and need to step back and look at higher values objectively.

Suggestions that might help

The availability of spiritual support is often outside the reach of many older people. It is therefore highly important that those around them take the initiative and either provide that support or facilitate its provision. In some cases this might include taking older neighbours, relatives or friends to Mass. In some areas, parish groups are in place that will visit the housebound and provide spiritual care (see Society of St Simon of Cyrene, in 'Useful Contacts and Helplines'). Spirituality resources in the form of CDs or DVDs are available that can be used by people individually or in groups, in day care or in nursing homes (see appendices). Serenity Spirituality Sessions require a facilitator to lead the group. These group sessions can provide spiritual care in an effective way, especially if Mass is not available. It is important for the person who manages the nursing home to understand the spiritual needs of residents and provide facilities so that spirituality sessions are available for residents. A variety of other spirituality resources can be found in religious and parish book shops.

On television, EWTN regularly televises Mass, as do other stations. Also when the Pope is on foreign travels, EWTN (and sometimes Sky News) cover his visits extensively.

Providing older people with the symbols of religion that were meaningful to them in the past will have a positive impact. Just to be able to hold rosary beads, or to be blessed with holy water, can provide a considerable measure of comfort. To pray with them or to pray for other people that they love is also meaningful. In their own home they might like a Christmas crib or a May altar but would need assistance in producing these. Care needs to be exercised in relation to candles and the dangers associated with naked flames, especially in nursing homes where for safety reasons they may be forbidden. Battery candles can help in that case.

Day-to-day care of older people can take on a spiritual dimension if done with kindness and respect. Making time to really listen to what the older person needs to say is in itself a spiritual activity; spiritual care includes being treated with respect.

Finally, helping to create an uplifting environment for the older person with suitably selected pictures, statues, flowers and lights that are safe will add greatly to the joy of many older people.

Spiritual well-being can be introduced through music, poetry, reflective sessions focused on nature, or beauty as experienced by any of the senses. These sessions can be an addition to formal prayer sessions or can be provided on their own for residents who do not have a formal church affiliation.

Finding ourselves and our related spiritual challenges in the gospels

When Jesus was hot and tired he sat down at the well in Samaria, he was joined by a woman with whom he started to have a conversation *(John 4:20)*. Her reputation wasn't the best but Jesus accepted her unconditionally and in this incident he shared who he was in a way that he had not done before. Jesus showed great respect for ordinary people in many of the incidents where he performed miracles. He also taught his disciples to pray when he gave them the Our Father *(Luke 11:1-13)*.

Imagine you are also at the well in Samaria. The woman leaves and now it is your turn to talk to Jesus. Listen to what he might say about himself and wait until he asks you to tell him who you are and what your dreams are. In the other incident, he taught his disciples to say the Our Father. Maybe say this prayer with him and ask him to help you whenever you find it difficult to pray.

Then you play your part by living with the situation as it effects you in the present and either asking for the grace to be patient while you wait for things to improve or thanking God for the way you have been helped by others. It can be helpful to adopt the attitude of allowing yourself to feel the discomfort of the relative absence of spiritual care instead of fighting against it. That can lead to greater acceptance which, in turn, can contribute to a resolution of your problem, if there is a problem.

⟿ SECTION 6 ⟿
How do challenges in later life make you feel?

In general terms, problematic issues can make you feel sad due to, amongst other things, loss of loved ones or of your own independence. Boredom can give you too much time for negative reflection. Hearing loss and difficulty, eyesight or memory problems can be distressing. Spiritually, reduced access to church services can be saddening for many people whose lives were closely bound up with their local parish community.

Perhaps you feel angry because of what you perceive as a lack of respect or consideration of your needs from others. The poor maintenance of public areas is a challenge to those with reduced mobility and accessing public services can be sufficiently challenging to make older people angry. Attitudes in society such as abortion, gay marriage or dismissive or disrespectful attitudes to older people with disabilities such as dementia can cause great distress. Generalisations can make older people feel angry, since many in the older age group are still able to participate extensively in wider community life. Spiritually, people feel angry when their needs are not met, when they are housebound and are left without spiritual care, or when they are not housebound but have lost many of the Masses and other services that had been available to them. Hearing their faith spoken of disrespectfully, especially on radio or TV, is very distressing for some older people.

At the top of the list, in terms of inducing happiness,

is relationships. This can be relationships within your own family, including between grandparents and grandchildren, and also when families are considerate towards older people and include them where possible in family activities. For older people, they can be ecstatic even when they eventually find a hearing aid that works for them, or are referred for cataract surgery after which their sight improves. Older people are spiritually happy when they get the opportunity to pray with others, using the old familiar prayers and joining in with old familiar hymns such as those provided by the Ciúnas or Serenity Spirituality Sessions (see appendices).

Communication as a Challenge in Later Life

A writer on the subject of communication in older people had this to say:

> Communication is a basic ingredient in successful living across the lifespan. At a time of life that we may be influenced by negative stereotyping and filled with unparalleled changes, including those involved with health, mental and social status, communication assumes a prominent role in the well-being of all older people.
>
> — Rosemary Lubinski,
> *Dementia and Communication, 1995.*

Here I will try to identify practical communication difficulties in later life and, as far as possible, what can be done about them. It is a known fact that several features of communication are affected by the ageing process, for example: forgetting or not being able to access names or appropriate words (the 'senior moment'), mild short-term memory loss which makes us repeat ourselves, forgetting that we have already shared a piece of information; we use more pronouns and fewer nouns, 'she' or 'he' instead of the person's name, 'the thing' or 'it' instead of the proper name of an object; as our hearing deteriorates we can begin to talk more loudly and perhaps develop the habit of asking people to repeat what they have said; our dental condition (including absence of some, or many, teeth) can affect our pronunciation as can poor muscle tone of tongue, lips, palate. We may be a bit shorter of breath due to respiratory conditions and this can affect volume so that we can't be heard very well. On the whole, we can be slower and less effective in how we speak.

We can look at how we communicate without speaking at all, and how non-verbal factors affect the communication process. Non-verbal, in this context, refers to communicating without using words.

The most obvious non-verbal communication is *silence* and this can be used positively or negatively. There are various ways in which silence can be used positively. Rather than saying something one might regret it can be wiser to say nothing – a piece of advice often adopted after learning the hard way. Another positive use is in the context of close relationships. When people are really close, they don't need to keep talking in order to feel comfortable. Instead they can enjoy a companionable silence.

That being said, silence *can* be used as a punishment. Children can be heard to say, 'I'm not talking to you'. Sometimes the child within the adult surfaces and, without a declared intention, the silent treatment can be adopted. We know that the Bible tells us not to let the sun go down on our anger. Could silence be an unconscious way of giving expression to that anger? Are there not more adult (and effective) ways of doing that?

Many older people experience some level of sustained low mood. When a person is so inflicted, their energy level can be so low that they are not motivated to take part in ordinary social conversation, even to the point of being unable to communicate. Their silence can be misinterpreted, instead of being recognised as an alerting sign that something needs to be done and attended-to by a professional in the field. Another feature of depression is irritability, usually shown in tone of voice and body language. We need to make allowances for that person and remember that everybody has their own story.

Tone of voice is a powerful form of non-verbal communication. It can be used to give extra weight to any emotion. We all remember angry (or frustrated, rather) teachers or other significant adults who used a tone of voice that put the 'fear of God' into us. Maybe we never got over the feeling of anxiety that an angry tone of voice evoked in us, so that we are still oversensitive to authority figures who intimidate us too easily by the way they address us.

Maybe we know some people who speak with a quiver in their voice showing their fear or lack of self-confidence. This gives us a chance to be a peacemaker, to enhance that person's self-esteem and help to free them from this form of suffering.

A calm or soothing tone of voice can provide much comfort in bereavement or loss or when somebody is lonely or upset. A singing voice can, in some instances, provide that kind of comfort but normal conversational voice is best if it sounds reassuring and understanding. A problem arises when the person being spoken to is deaf. It is difficult to raise one's volume without sounding as if we are shouting. The intention behind the increased volume, as well as modulating how we sound, is what matters.

Eye contact, facial expression or other forms of body language are powerful non-verbal communicators. I once saw a smile described as, 'A look of love, freely given'. We all know the difference between somebody who, in greeting us, gives us their full attention with a smile, rather than looking over our shoulder as they shake our hand while making eye contact with somebody else. In the first case we feel respected but not in the second. We sometimes forget that, just as we can be affected by other people's non-verbal communication they too can be affected by ours.

It is useful to reflect upon how we behave as listeners as well as speakers. As a listener, do I give my full attention to the person who is speaking to me? Hearing loss makes this more difficult but even so, it is necessary to be focused on the speaker rather than letting attention wander. As a listener, do I allow for the amount of time the other person has available to communicate with me. This is particularly relevant in the nursing home situation where staff are genuinely busy.

Am I listened to? A factor in whether I am or not is my ability to articulate my concerns in an effective manner; speech has a number of different functions so do I need to say how I feel, to ask questions, to express preferences and choices, or share my worries and my joys? Do I need to say when I have had enough or to ask for more or to refuse something when offered? These are some of the many functions of language which display how necessary it is to be a conscientious speaker in order to ensure you are listened to by others.

The following shows the effects of poor communication or not being listened to, 'When a person is unable to communicate adequately and effectively, the capacity for relationships is reduced, the achievement of potential inhibited, and the impact on quality of life may be enormous' (Margaret Leahy, *Disorders of Communication*, 1995). St Ireneus reminded us that, 'The Glory of God is the human person fully alive'. Healthy relationships, built on effective communication, can go a long way to honouring the potential of each older person.

Pope John XXIII encouraged us to pray to 'unite all minds in truth and all hearts in charity'. This reminds us that in speaking bluntly we need to remember charity, so as not to cause unnecessary hurt, and that sometimes it is better to refrain from making a comment or giving certain information as it is not always necessary or positive to do so.

Challenges around Going into Care

As a person ages, they often need support to continue to live well in their own home. The key challenges here are the person's physical and mental health, the type of home in which they live, their living arrangements, the availability of family and social supports and their financial resources. The same challenges apply whether a person is living alone, with family or in a group setting. Where an older person is a carer, they are especially in need of support if they and the person they are caring for are to continue to be able to live at home. Every effort should be made to support the older person to remain at home as long as possible.

(a) Continuing to live at home

Considerations from the point of view of the elderly:

∼ They will maintain freedom and independence, and live according to their own preferences and choices.
∼ They must have sufficient financial resources to pay for any home care that might be needed.
∼ Their family should play an active role in supporting them to live as independently as they wish; the person may be living with, or close to, other family members.
∼ They should have good social supports, with some

close friends or neighbours whom they see regularly.

- ➤ They should be sufficiently well, so as not to need specialised medical interventions; they are not cognitively impaired.
- ➤ They should either live on one level (a bungalow or apartment), or their two-storey home can be adapted to facilitate their needs.
- ➤ They should have access to transport and someone to accompany them to attend medical and other appointments.

Considerations from the point of view of the family:

- ➤ They should be actively supportive, and have sufficient resources (time, financial resources) to respond to the older person's needs.
- ➤ They should take all possible safety precautions including the fitting of a personal safety alarm, a telephone that the older person can manage, a house alarm, a smoke alarm, and make arrangements to ensure the availability of immediate personal help should it be needed in a crisis.
- ➤ There should be sufficient backup from extended family; often, when a person's support needs are high, family members have a rota to ensure continuity of support.
- ➤ They should make the necessary adaptations to the person's home to make it more suitable for the person's needs.

(b) Moving to residential care

Considerations from the point of view of the older person:

- They can no longer live at home because their living arrangements, family and social supports, and available financial resources do not make it possible.
- Their freedom, independence and autonomy is curtailed, to varying degrees, in residential care.
- As a nursing home resident, their choices and preferences may not be considered adequately. They lose the familiarity of what they have been used to.
- They are at risk of feeling lonely and isolated in the nursing home, unless they have frequent visits from family and/or friends. This is particularly true if they have to leave pets behind.
- They may be kept waiting when they need attention, or staff may not be able to give them the time they need to function at their own pace, if the nursing home is not well staffed.
- The quality of life in nursing homes is very variable; with the best providing a 'home-from-home' that is comfortable, flexible, responsive to the resident's preferences and choices, and has opportunities for social and recreational activities.

Considerations from the point of view of the family:

- They are not in a position to provide the level of support that the person needs because of personal or other family commitments, or other reasons.

- They don't live nearby and so can't provide immediate assistance should the person need it.
- They may not have sufficient backup from other family members.

When making the decision

Should a decision be made that the older person should move to a care setting, a careful transition plan should be put in place. Unfortunately, this is often not possible as the person's transition into long-term care may be made straight from the acute hospital following illness or accident.

This highlights the need for families to have a discussion with their loved one *in advance of any decision making*, so that the older person's wishes are made known and taken into account as much as possible.

CONCLUSION

This booklet has been published to share experiences and add to our collective basic knowledge and awareness of challenges in later life, as well as informing us of alternative ways of coping and coming to terms with the difficulties that arise in later years. We have drawn on scripture to see how Jesus dealt with people's difficulties and found examples in the gospels where Jesus intervened. It does not claim to explore the complexity of all real life issues but it is hoped that you, the reader, will find echoes of your own personal experiences and find encouragement in what you have read.

⫷ Active Retirement Ireland

For those who are still active, you will find an active retirement group in or near your local area. There are branches throughout the country. Alternatively, there may be a senior choir in your area that you could join.

The Capel Buildings, St Mary's Abbey, Dublin.

Phone: 01 8733836.

⫷ Alone

This is not a helpline, but they offer a befriending service through their 150 volunteers. These include people who will see to a leaking roof, fix a broken cooker or do other practical jobs. They also provide a list of other befriending services.

Olympic House, Pleasants Street, Saint Kevin's, Dublin.

Phone: 01 6791032

⫷ The Alzheimer Society of Ireland

Their services include a national helpline, social clubs, support groups, day care, home care, respite centres and much more.

Temple Road, Blackrock, Dublin.

Phone: 01 2073800

⫷ Friends of the Elderly

This is an Irish volunteer based charity established in 1980 to bring friendship and companionship to older people living alone or who feel lonely.

25 Bolton Street, Dublin 1.

Phone: 01 8731855; email: info@friendsoftheelderly.ie

✍ The Irish Heart Foundation

This organisation will provide you with any information you may need about stroke or heart attack.

50 Ringsend Road, Dublin.

Phone: 01 6685001

✍ The Irish Hospice Foundation

It is important for older people to think ahead. The IHF have helpful guidance about advance directives, which are a way of seeing that your wishes for the future are still respected when you are not in a position to plan for yourself.

Morrison Chambers, Nassau Street, Dublin 2.

Phone: 01 6793188.

✍ Later Life Mediation

There is a cost involved in this service. Trained staff can be asked 'to facilitate difficult conversations'. They can be useful around family difficulties about property or inheritance.

13 Fitzwilliam Place, Dublin 2.

Phone: 01 6856747; email: info@laterlifemediation.com

✍ SAGE

This is a support and advocacy service for older people. Its mission is 'to promote and protect the rights, freedoms and dignity of older people by developing support and advocacy services wherever ageing poses a challenge for individuals.'

24 Ormond Quay Upper, Inns Quay, Dublin 7.

Phone: 01 5367330 or 1850 71 9400;

email: info@sage.thirdageireland.ie

⤙ Senior Helpline

This is a phone-based support service. The volunteer who answers the phone begins by questioning why the caller is lonely, and will make suggestions as to how to meet other people in the same situation.

The Third Age Foundation, New Road,
Summerhill, Meath.
Phone: 046 9557766.

⤙ The Society of St Simon of Cyrene

This group was set up in 2000 to provide company for housebound people in a given parish. Volunteers are assigned to visit and engage spiritually with parishioners who are not able to get to the parish church. It has spread to other parishes.

Phone: 01 2884009 (mornings only)

⤙ The St Vincent de Paul Society

SVP work to combat loneliness via its system of personal visitation, services such as day centres, social housing and holidays and the provision of personal alarms. Local branches of the society can be contacted through your nearest parish.

91-92 Sean MacDermott Street, Dublin 1
Phone: 01 8386990.

For any readers with internet access, you can find further information on all the organisations mentioned above online.

The Ciúnas Collection and *Serenity Spirituality Sessions* are services that are offered by the author, Sr Mary Threadgold.

THE CIÚNAS COLLECTION

The Ciúnas Collection is a traditional series of Catholic hymns and prayers for older people in residential or home care, including those living with Alzheimer's.

These are prayers that were once familiar to all older Catholics when prayers were a regular feature in their lives. Without these prayers, there is something missing in day-to-day life; with them their spiritual well-being is enhanced.

The CDs are designed to connect with the emotional and spiritual feelings of peace and calmness as the prayers and hymns are recited and reflected upon. Ciúnas means stillness and quietness, this is the spiritual contentedness experienced by participants of the Ciúnas Collection.

There is a booklet included that explains the rationale behind the use of Ciúnas and the benefits that have been observed when it is used. It gives tips to help facilitators, especially those in nursing homes, to use the approach effectively as well as suggesting ways of enhancing the use of the CDs. This booklet also provides the words of the hymns and prayers used throughout the Ciúnas sessions.

There is a DVD included to support a broader sense of

spirituality. Spirituality includes a relationship with the created world, and the uplifting scenery is pleasant to watch while viewers reflect.

How to get it

You can get more information via the following details:

Web: www.sonasapc.ie

Phone: 01 2608138

Email: info@sonasapc.ie

SERENITY SPIRITUALITY SESSIONS

As people get older, many find great comfort in the prayers and hymns that they once knew. This is especially true of those whose memory is failing, who are in residential care or housebound. Spiritual needs in this group of people are not always met.

The Serenity Spirituality Sessions box set is a way for older people of any Christian denomination to pray with a group of likeminded people. Sessions are led by a facilitator and last approximately forty-five minutes. They include hymns and prayers, scripture reading, time to reflect and time to pray for others (and to be prayed for) in a quiet environment that includes a nature display.

How to get it

You can get more information via the following details:

Web: www.sonasapc.ie

Phone: 01 2608138

Email: info@sonasapc.ie

SPIRITUAL REMINISCENCE

Since 2006, Elizabeth Mackinlay, an Australian nurse, academic, and Anglican minister has added greatly to our awareness of a tool which can be used to enhance meaning in life for older people. Spiritual Reminiscence is a way of telling a life story with emphasis on meaning. It can identify meaning associated with joy, sadness, anger, guilt, or regret. Exploring these issues in older age can help people to reframe some of these events and come to a new understanding of the meaning and purpose of their lives. She suggests using questions such as:

- What gives you most meaning in your life?
- What does spirituality mean for you?
- What makes you feel happy or sad?
- What has brought you joy?
- What do you look forward to as you come near the end of your life?

Sessions can be carried out with individuals or small groups but need a facilitator who is familiar with this kind of work. When carried out in small groups, the participants get to know one another in a new way. She suggests that the skills that are needed to lead reminiscence groups effectively are no different to the skills used in personal support professions, namely: listening, generosity with time and the ability to give feedback.

For anybody interested in learning more about Elizabeth

Mackinlay's work, look up her publications, especially *Facilitating Spiritual Reminiscence for People with Dementia: A Learning Guide* (2015) and, *Spiritual Growth and Care in the Fourth Age of Life* (2006).